What Is a Blizzard?

Robin Johnson

Crabtree Publishing Company
www.crabtreebooks.com

Author: Robin Johnson

Publishing plan research and development: Reagan Miller

Editors: Reagan Miller and Janine Deschenes

Proofreaders: Kathy Middleton and Petrice Custance

Design and photo research: Samara Parent

Prepress technician: Samara Parent

Print and production coordinator: Kathy Berti

Photographs

Associated Press: p15 © AP Photo/Michael Conroy
Getty Images: p9 © Digital Light Source
iStock: contents page; p4; p5 © fodera72; p10; p11; p12; p17
Shutterstock: title page © Jaminnbenji

All other images from Shutterstock

About the author

Robin Johnson has written more than 60 educational books for children. She plans to keep writing books and chasing rainbows—whatever the weather.

Library and Archives Canada Cataloguing in Publication

Johnson, Robin (Robin R.), author
        What is a blizzard? / Robin Johnson.

(Severe weather close-up)
Includes index.
Issued in print and electronic formats.
ISBN 978-0-7787-2395-0 (bound).--ISBN 978-0-7787-2425-4
(paperback).--ISBN 978-1-4271-1748-9 (html)

        1. Blizzards--Juvenile literature. I. Title.

QC926.37.J65 2016   j551.55'5   C2015-908674-4
                                          C2015-908675-2

Library of Congress Cataloging-in-Publication Data

CIP available at the Library of Congress

Crabtree Publishing Company

Printed in Canada/032016/EF20160210

www.crabtreebooks.com   1-800-387-7650

Published in Canada
Crabtree Publishing
616 Welland Ave.
St. Catharines, Ontario
L2M 5V6

Published in the United States
Crabtree Publishing
PMB 59051
350 Fifth Avenue, 59th Floor
New York, New York 10118

Published in the United Kingdom
Crabtree Publishing
Maritime House
Basin Road North, Hove
BN41 1WR

Published in Australia
Crabtree Publishing
3 Charles Street
Coburg North
VIC 3058

Contents

Snow day

Have you ever played in snow? It is white and fluffy. It feels cold. You can make snowmen or slide down snowy hills. Snow is fun! But it can also be dangerous.

The weather

Snow is part of the **weather**. Weather is what the air and sky are like in a certain place at a certain time. Sunlight, **wind**, and **temperature** are other parts of weather. Wind is moving air. Temperature is how warm or cold the air is.

Different weather

Different places get different weather. Many parts of the world have four **seasons**. A season is a time of year that has a certain kind of weather. The seasons are winter, spring, summer, and fall. Each season has a **weather pattern**. For example, it may be rainy in the spring, hot and sunny in the summer, cool in the fall, and cold and snowy in the winter.

What do you Think?

Describe the weather pattern of each season where you live.

Falling water

Places with very cold winters can get snow. Snow is a form of **precipitation**. Precipitation is water that falls from clouds. Rain and **hail** are other kinds of precipitation.

How is snow made?

The Sun heats air near the ground. The air rises, cools, and forms tiny water droplets high in the sky. The droplets join together to form clouds. When the temperature is warm, water falls from the clouds as rain. When the temperature is very cold, the water freezes and falls as snow.

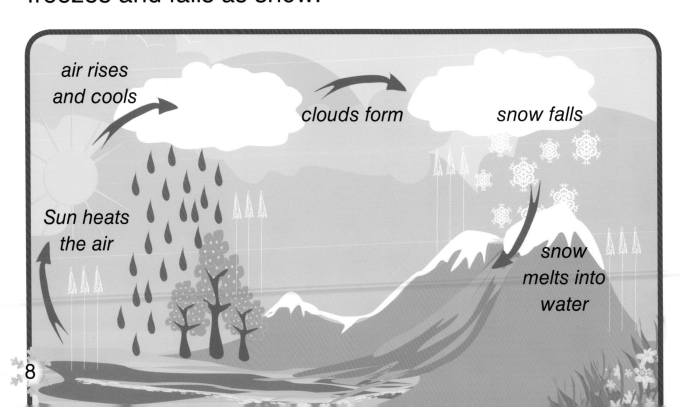

air rises and cools

clouds form

snow falls

Sun heats the air

snow melts into water

Snowstorms

When a lot of snow falls, it is called a **snowstorm**. Some snowstorms last for just a few hours. Other snowstorms last for days. The snow builds up over time. It covers the ground like a giant white blanket.

What do you Think?

*This girl is using a **thermometer** to measure the temperature. What clues in this picture tell you that it is cold outside?*

What is a blizzard?

A **blizzard** is a huge snowstorm with very strong winds. The wind blows snow all around. Blizzards can cause **whiteouts**. A whiteout is when blowing snow makes it very hard to see. All you can see is white! The temperature is very cold during blizzards. The wind makes it feel even colder. Brrrr!

During blizzards, wind blows snow into tall piles called **snowdrifts**. *Snowdrifts can cover street signs, cars, and even parts of buildings!*

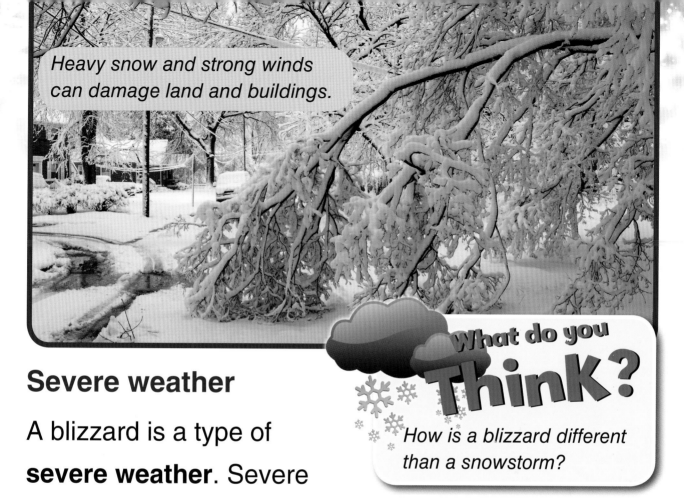

Heavy snow and strong winds can damage land and buildings.

Severe weather

What do you **Think?**

How is a blizzard different than a snowstorm?

A blizzard is a type of **severe weather**. Severe weather is weather that can be harmful to people and animals. Freezing temperatures and strong winds can make blizzards dangerous. If a person becomes stuck or lost in the blowing snow, the extreme cold can cause **frostbite**. Frostbite is a severe injury to the skin.

When and where?

Blizzards can happen anytime from early fall to late spring. In North America, most blizzards happen in January and February. The weather is usually coldest during these months. Blizzards can happen in any place that has cold winter weather, such as the United States, Canada, and Russia.

Blizzards are more likely to happen where the land is mostly flat and there are not many trees. Without trees to block the wind, winds can become fast and strong.

Blizzard Alley

In the United States, blizzards are most common in the Great Plains and Upper Midwest regions. In Canada, areas in the far north, prairie provinces, and provinces along the Atlantic Ocean get the most blizzards.

On this map, snowflakes show where blizzards happen most in North America. In the United States, the states with snowflakes make up an area known as "Blizzard Alley."

Weather warnings

Meteorologists warn us about blizzards so we can stay safe. Meteorologists are scientists who study weather. They measure wind, snow, temperature, and other parts of weather. They use this information to **predict** when blizzards might happen. To predict means to tell what may happen in the future.

*A blizzard **warning** is sent out when snow and winds of 35 mph or more are expected to last at least 3 hours. In Canada, it is winds of 40 kph lasting at least 4 hours.*

Be prepared

Meteorologists warn people when blizzards are expected in an area. This helps people prepare for the weather and stay safe. People can learn about the weather reports in their area on television or online. They can listen to weather reports on the radio, too.

What do you Think?

Why is it important to know when blizzards are coming?

BLIZZARD WARNING
NORTH OF INDPLS
TRAVEL DISCOURAGED

WEATHER ALERT

15

Stay indoors

You should stay indoors when blizzards happen. Drink plenty of water, juice, and warm liquids. Eat regular meals. Food gives your body **energy** to make its own heat. Energy is the power needed to do things.

Remember to bring your pets indoors if there is a blizzard warning.

Play it safe

During a blizzard, heavy snow can pile on top of electricity wires. This can cause you to lose power and heat in your home. Make sure you have flashlights handy in case the lights go out. Bundle up to stay warm. Wear layers of loose, lightweight, warm clothing. Wrap yourself in cozy blankets. Read books, do puzzles, or play board games to pass the time.

What do you Think?

Why is it unsafe to be outside during blizzards?

After the storm

Make sure the blizzard is over before you go outdoors. You can check a weather report to find out. If you lost power in your house, you can listen to a report using a radio that runs on batteries or wait until the power is back on. There will be a lot of snow outside your home. Grab a shovel and help your family dig out!

Check on your neighbors to make sure they are safe. Then help them shovel, too!

Bundle up!

The weather will still be freezing cold after the storm ends, so dress warmly to go outside. Put on a winter coat, snow pants, mittens, and a hat that covers your ears. Wear warm, **waterproof** winter boots that do not slip. Sidewalks may be icy.

Get ready!

Even animals in cold regions get ready for winter. They gather food. They grow thick fur. They make cozy homes. You can get ready for winter, too! Make a blizzard kit to help keep you safe during a blizzard.

Make a list

During a blizzard, you might be **snowed in** for more than a day. Being snowed in means you are not able to leave your home. What if your home lost power and heat? Cold temperatures can also cause water pipes to freeze. This may mean you cannot get water from your taps. If these things happened, how would you stay warm? What would you eat and drink? Write a list of items you might need in a blizzard kit. Check your list against the one on the next page.

You should plan to have enough supplies to stay at home for three days without power or heat.

21

Winter storm kit

This list shows some items in a winter storm kit. Help your family gather the supplies you need.

Checklist
- ✓ first aid kit
- ✓ radio that runs on batteries
- ✓ extra batteries
- ✓ flashlights
- ✓ waterproof matches
- ✓ bottled water (enough for at least three days)
- ✓ canned food and other food that does not spoil (enough for at least three days)
- ✓ a can opener
- ✓ extra blankets
- ✓ warm clothing
- ✓ books, games, and other activities

Learning more

Books

Blizzards by Cari Meister. Jump!, 2015.

Changing Weather: Storms by Kelley MacAulay and Bobbie Kalman. Crabtree Publishing Company, 2006.

Snowstorm by Jim Mezzanotte. Weekly Reader Early Learning, 2009.

Winter Storm or Blizzard? by Kelly Doudna. Super Sandcastle, 2016.

Websites

This useful fact sheet tells you how to prepare and stay safe during severe winter weather:
www.ready.gov/kids/know-the-facts/winter-storms-extreme-cold#

Learn more about winter storms and other severe weather at:
www.weatherwizkids.com/weather-winter-storms.htm

Take a quiz, read a story, do an activity, and learn more about blizzards at:
https://eo.ucar.edu/kids/dangerwx/blizzard1.htm

Learn about snow, temperature, wind, the seasons, and more at:
http://extension.illinois.edu/treehouse/clouds.cfm?Slide=8

Words to know

Note: Some boldfaced words are defined where they appear in the book.

blizzard (BLIZ-erd) noun A huge snowstorm with strong winds

frostbite (FRAWST-bahyt) noun An injury to skin caused by cold temperatures

hail (HEYL) noun Hard chunks of ice that fall from clouds

predict (pri-DIKT) verb To tell what will happen before it takes place

snowstorm (SNOH-stawrm) noun A heavy fall of snow

temperature (TEHM-per-a-chur) noun A measure of how hot or cold something is

thermometer (ther-MOM-i-ter) noun A tool used to measure temperature

warning (WAWR-ning) noun A notice that alerts people to possible danger

waterproof (WAW-ter-proof) adjective Not allowing water to go through

weather pattern (WETH-er PAT-ern) noun Repeating weather, usually during different seasons

A noun is a person, place, or thing. A verb is an action word that tells you what someone or something does. An adjective is a word that tells you what something is like.

Index